Expert Secrets — Self-Discipline

The Ultimate Guide to Develop Daily Habits, Emotional Control, Focus, Mental Toughness, Self-Confidence, and Willpower for Happiness, Success, Weight Loss, and at Work

Terry Lindberg

Table of Contents

Hey, it's Terry Lindberg,

Before we start, I want to tell you about an exclusive offer just for readers of this book...

When starting your self-help journey, the one thing that you must have in check is your mindset. If your mindset is not up to scratch you are setting yourself up for failure before you have even started.

To have the mindset shift that you'll need to set you up for success; you have to do endless amounts of research to get mental clarity, acquire new daily habits, and much more.

Sounds like hard work, right?

Well yes, it would be, but luckily for you, I have partnered up with Intelligence Mastery. Who are giving away their highly rated course that will give you all of the step-by-step process for shifting your mindset into gear seamlessly!

Best thing about this exclusive offer is it 100% FREE, no-strings-attached. Intelligence Mastery usually charge $297 for this exact same course to their customers

All you need to do to claim your FREE the Ultimate Mindset Course; is in your search browsers URL go to – free.intelligencemastery.com

Once you are on the web page, fill out the required information that Intelligence Mastery asks for; this should only take less than 1 minute of your time. Then straight away in your email inbox you will receive the life changing course that has helped 10,000's of people around the world.

Before reading any further, please do this NOW as I may refer back to some of the units in the course throughout this book!

free.intelligencemastery.com

Who Is Terry Lindberg?

Hello, and Thank you for purchasing a copy from the "Expert Secrets – Self Help Series."

For all of you who do not know who I am, my name is Terry Lindberg, an award-winning Psychologist and Author of the Expert Secrets – Self Help Series. I have dedicated 30+ years of my entire life for innovating the field of psychology and self-help to improve mine and 1000's of other's lives across the globe ranging from top CEO's in their area to the best athletes, and even just regular individuals.

The one thing I can say about everyone who I have worked with is that they see dramatic changes in their lives following my teachings. My teachings help them to push through barriers they never thought they could get through. In most cases, the same outcome happens; they witness a switch go off in their mind, showing them the human brain is far more powerful than they could ever think was imaginable.

Throughout the entire 30+ years of my life studying in the field of psychology and self-help, I have acquired wisdom and unique experiences from the people who I have worked alongside and interviewed. The vast amount of knowledge that I have gained is everything that I will be passing onto you within this book.

This guide is not like any other self-help book out there, as to be honest 99% of self-help books on the market are not even made by someone within the field. They have partnered up with a ghost-writer to produce the contents of the book, then packaged and marketed to you as if it was made by someone who has experience in that topic.

The information that I will share with you has proof of concept and will actually assist you at whatever point you are on your journey.

Have you ever heard of the theory "The Golden Nugget" when reading a book? This theory means that an entire book could be irrelevant to the topic, but yet there could be one "Golden Nugget" of information that could be life-changing.

Because of this theory, I want you to be prepared and make sure for the length of this entire book that I have your full attention. By the way, if you didn't notice that the sentence before said "the" back to back, you're not paying enough attention.

Drop everything you are doing, focus on in, and be prepared to take notes. You may be only one sentence away from changing your life forever.

If you learn or like anything about the content, you have consumed when finished. An honest review is always appreciated for helping me make better content in the future.

Now let's get started...

Introduction

When was the last time you acted on impulse? Was it at work when you chose to end the day early even though your to-do list was still full? Did you decide to have that fourth, fifth, or sixth slice of pizza even though you promised yourself your diet would start today? Have you ever decided to skip the gym, call in "sick," or procrastinate a project on an impulse?

Everyone has these moments of weakness from time to time. A fun life allows a little impulsivity.

An issue can start to occur when the pattern of acting on impulse becomes the main deciding factor for what actions to take next. A lack of self-discipline can present many problems for those struggling to create willpower.

It's stressful to stay organized, stick to a schedule, and constantly motivate yourself to do more. What causes us even more prolonged anxiety is avoiding these things altogether.

We all have moments where we naturally say "no" to ourselves. Maybe someone makes you angry and you want to say something insulting, only to remind yourself that "it'll only make things worse" if you do decide to speak up. Perhaps you say "no" to checking out after adding $200 to your online shopping cart, knowing the money is better spent going toward paying off bills.

Self-discipline is easy in some cases because of our ability to quickly weigh the consequences in our minds. Buying a bunch of stuff you don't need is always fun, but doing it too much while ignoring other finances can be disastrous.

You already have self-discipline. It's naturally built into the way you operate because it protects us. A delicious fruit on the top of a tree looks appealing to the hungry eye, but your mind will also point out the dangers there if you decide to climb to the top. You'll assess the branches to climb up and the potential fall, while also factoring your own physical ability to have the strength to climb.

This ability to gauge a situation is a survival tactic. A cat will look at where they are about to jump and only do so if they fully believe they'll be available to have a smooth landing. This isn't always the result, but that leap isn't done blindly initially. A dog will still smell something before eating it. This doesn't stop them from eating things they shouldn't in all situations, but it still protects them from certain things.

While this self-discipline is a natural part of us, sometimes it might just not be strong enough. Think of it like a muscle. Most can lift a glass to their mouths to take a drink. Not everyone could lift a 100-pound dumbbell, however. The more you work on building your self-discipline, the easier it is to have these thoughts and desires under control.

A 2011 survey in the U.S. determined 1 out of 4 people agreed that having low self-discipline was the reason they continued to struggle with success in reference to making healthier choices (Raving, 2019).

Self-discipline can help you:

- Gain more focus
- Increase emotional control
- Boost self-confidence
- Strengthen willpower

Throughout my more than 30 years working with different patients and diving into their thoughts, the truth has become clearer: **It is our own mind that continues to set us up for failure.** There are triggers that cause us to act impulsively all around us, but the power still lies within our own hands.

It's easy to struggle with self-discipline as a human, but especially as one living in our world now. Impulsivity has become a natural way of life. Your phone is a constant form of entertainment. There is an endless amount of information online. We can think up and chase any sort of topic we want. You can scroll social media and read other people's thoughts all day long. You can play games and even spend money on them. You can read articles and watch videos. You can talk to friends and strangers from across the world. All of this can be done without us even realizing we've spent two hours procrastinating work.

These triggers cause you so many problems. They can keep you too distracted to work. You might read something that makes you upset, leaving you feeling sad the rest of the day. These triggers can be so small, but they can set the course for the rest of our day, or even week, if we're not using self-discipline.

The biggest roadblock to self-discipline is your mentality. Even though these external triggers sometimes feel like they have the power, you are the one who made the decision to act on impulse. For example, how many times have you said, "I couldn't help it because of X reason." That reason might have been the influence of a friend, the reminder of something you saw online, or a seemingly uncontrollable feeling like anger or hunger. Even though it might appear these things have the control, at the end of the day, you are still the one who will always be in charge.

It doesn't take a psychologist to know that mental toughness will be beneficial in anyone's life. The problem is, many don't know how to strengthen their minds. In this book, I want to show you small habits and how retraining your thoughts doesn't have to be a painful process. With the right mindset tools, cultivating a life of mental strength will feel natural, making you wish you'd taken these steps sooner.

According to a 2008 study, those who have self-control are shown to:

- Have better grades
- Have healthier relationships
- Be less likely to have alcohol dependence or binge eating disorders
- Have better emotional management (Baumeister, Boone, & Tangney, 2008).

Most of us can easily see the benefits of increased self-control. The issue arises with our inability to emulate the qualities that one with a refined internal discipline has.

Self-control exists in the mind. The more power you give to external circumstances, the less control you give yourself. The power to be successful, healthy, and happy is inside the organ between your two ears.

Chapter 1: Success Stories

What kind of expert would I be if I didn't offer evidence of my help in the past? Below are two different stories of people (who gave permission to share) who have managed to change their life around by using my teachings of self-discipline.

A Change in Career

Steven was a patient of mine who was very intelligent but had almost no motivation.

He had dreams of being a writer, but anyone in the field knows it's not an easy job. The biggest thing blocking him along the way was himself. He had the talent, education, and experience. He shared some pieces he'd written with me, and I could see he had a unique way of bringing the page to life.

The problem was that he didn't want to *practice* writing. He thought everything he created was supposed to be a unique, one-of-a-kind masterpiece. We'd come up with a writing schedule for him to follow week to week, and the first week, he did well. He was excited to wake up every day and get the stories in his head down on a page.

However, he'd always end up falling off track. He'd ignore his daily goals because he didn't have any strength or courage to keep writing. The thoughts of insecurity would plague his mind, making him feel like an utter disappointment if he wrote one wrong sentence or word.

On the outside, he was organized, put together, and successful as a schoolteacher. While he enjoyed this career, his true passion was to be an author one day. He ignored all his other successes and, instead, glued himself to the idea that he was a failure because he had not published a single thing yet.

In one of our weekly sessions, he had an epiphany. I asked him who his favorite author of all time was. Franz Kafka and Emily Dickinson came to mind. I couldn't help but chuckle to myself because both of these authors really only grew to fame and success after they had already died!

I asked him, "Out of all of Kafka's work, which is your favorite?" His response was he probably liked "The Castle" best. When looking over Kafka's entire career, this was one of his later novels.

I asked him, "Do you think Kafka gave up after a week of writing because he didn't create a masterpiece?"

This was enough to create a new mindset in him from that moment on. He was expecting every single thing he wrote to be brilliant without any edits or changes along the way. This was an unrealistic standard. Every person we admire has had moments of failure. For every great masterpiece, there are likely a few failed ones. Some might be uncovered decades from now through old discovered journals, but a big majority were likely thrown away right from the start.

Steven was disciplined enough to start writing but not enough to ignore the thoughts and anxieties and continue to push through. He could sit down to write but would never follow through. By working through those pressures and fears over his writing, we were able to create a schedule not just for creating new things but also for practicing his work and finding his voice.

The Key to Weight Loss

Ever since Deborah could remember, she'd been trying to lose weight.

Her first instance of wanting to shed the pounds was when she was just 12 years old. Some of the girls in her grade had begun hitting puberty, so they were developing curvier bodies. Her best friend at the time invited her to a pool party where everyone was wearing a bikini. Deborah was the only one to show up in a one-piece. From then on, she knew she wanted to be like every other girl who had been at the party with long, slim legs and a flat stomach.

When she was 16 years old, she bought her first bottle of diet pills. By the time she was 22, she had tried every diet fad out there, and yet she still couldn't stick to a healthier regimen.

She hated the way she looked in the mirror and would constantly say the worst things to herself.

Her diet was on the same cycle over and over again. She would start a new diet, not see results after a week, and then decide to give up. Sometimes, she might see a slight difference, but she hated every diet she tried, meaning it was hard to stick to it in the first place.

She was disciplined in her life with a great career and three healthy kids. The biggest problem she faced was the way she talked to herself.

One week, she tried a vegan diet, and by the third day, she'd caved and eaten a burger from the fast food restaurant around the corner. She came into my office and cried a few days later, talking about how that one sandwich set off a binge of junk food and other unhealthy choices.

The issue wasn't the lack of healthy options or even her desire to eat things that were good for her. The problem was her all-or-nothing thinking. She wasn't disciplined enough to stick to a diet because one minor mishap meant she had to give up.

We decided to come up with a new schedule for eating. We eliminated "diet" from her vocabulary and, instead, placed an emphasis on healthy eating and avoiding junk food as much as possible.

The trick was, she would give herself three cheats a week for the first month. This meant having a donut with breakfast, drinking a soda with dinner, or something else along those lines.

This way she could still have those crave-able foods without feeling like she had to give up on her new eating schedule.

Something miraculous happened next. She realized by doing this, she was giving herself permission. It was easier to stay disciplined because the pressure wasn't so heavy on her anymore.

She ended up not even using those three weekly cheats most of the time. She would feel so good about herself knowing she could still give in if she wanted, but instead, she trained her brain to think in a different way.

Finding a New Outlook

As a psychologist, I've seen a lot of people struggle with their own thoughts. What do Steven and Deborah have in common?

- They both wanted to change.
- They both put way too much pressure on themselves.

The issue for them, and most of us, is not that we lack self-discipline. We're just not using it in the *right* way.

Belittling yourself, calling yourself mean names, and being hard on yourself, in general, is not discipline! Though it might feel like you are giving yourself tough love, it's misguided. It ends up making us feel even worse, making it more challenging to want to pick up the pieces and keep going after a minor setback.

With patience and the use of self-discipline, success is achievable for everyone. Let's take a look next at what it truly means to have self-discipline.

Chapter 2: What Is Self-Discipline?

Self-discipline involves knowing the things that are within your control and choosing to take action as needed. Self-discipline involves your thoughts, emotions, actions, behavior, and reactions.

A lot of things are out of our control. We didn't get to pick who we were born to or where that occurred. We didn't get to pick the circumstances we were in as a child. There was no control over whether we were given abusive parents, loving parents, present parents, or neglectful parents. It wasn't within our boundary to choose what we were fed, what we were taught, and where we had to go to school and live.

The older we got, the more things came under our control. Eventually, we became in charge of the direction our lives went. We had been thrown so far one way for so long, it was hard to do a full 180. Some things were still, and would forever be, blocked off, but alternate paths always present themselves.

The same destination can have 100 different paths leading from it. The same path can branch off into 100 different destinations.

There will always be circumstances that are entirely out of our control. You can plan at a time when good weather is expected, but it might still rain. You can do your best to show up early, but you can't help it if there's a car accident in front of you on the road.

The Importance of Mental Strength

The one thing you do have power over? Your thoughts. No matter what happens, we still have some control over these thoughts. Your level of self-discipline will reflect how you're able to reign in these quickly passing ideas, responses, and behaviors. Some people seemingly have no control over their emotions. They might show this by lashing out at others, reacting poorly to bad news, responding too emotionally to pain, and so on.

Thoughts drive emotion. Emotion can drive impulse. Impulse creates our behavior, and that can be a huge contributing factor to where we end up in life. Someone who is always acting on impulse and unable to control their emotions might be making dangerous decisions. This could lead to a continuous cycle of mistakes, regrets, and negative results.

There will always be things that we don't have complete power over, and the things that run through our minds will always be one of those. For that reason, working out your mental strength is essential. Increasing your self-control means strengthening your ability to have more control over the rest of your life.

Signs of Weak Self-Discipline

Impulsivity can be beneficial. However, a life based around this can be a bigger sign of low self-discipline. It's fun to be able to say, "Sure, who cares," when a friend asks you to go out at night after you've already changed into your pajamas. You still have to wake up early, but you haven't seen this friend in a while, and it becomes a fun night where the two of you get to catch up. Doing this every night and always impulsively going out to bars might be more worrisome. Impulsively buying a dress on sale that you look great in can be fun, especially if you're someone who's always tight with the budget. However, impulsively shopping multiple times a day can lead to more disastrous problems.

Sometimes a lack of self-discipline can show in the ways you interact with others. Do you frequently have to apologize because you lashed out? Do you find it's common for people to be mad at you because you acted without considering them?

Finding you make the same mistakes over and over again might also be a lack of self-discipline. Always running late, always falling through with plans, never finishing a project, and having frequent feelings of being angry at yourself could show you're deeply struggling to keep things under control.

Creating goals but never following through with them can also show you're struggling to build your inner voice. It's easy to think up a million different goals, but fulfilling them and also seeing the results requires more than just imagination.

You might have success and still struggle internally. Are you always giving in to others' demands? Are you struggling to keep up with the things you've agreed to? Lacking self-discipline doesn't mean you're a failure! Many of us are functioning just fine on the outside, but internally, the endless pressures are hard to manage.

Why Do We Lack Self-Discipline?

A lack of self-discipline is mostly internal, but there's no denying the fact that there is a plethora of external circumstances working against you.

This includes marketing tactics used specifically to target impulsive decisions. BOGO (buy one, get one free) sales work well because you know that you don't need two things, or even one thing, but how can you resist getting a totally free thing? There are candy bars and sodas at the checkout station for a reason. It's easy to see these and think, "Only a few dollars, and I want a little snack anyway." Consider how often you seek these things out versus how frequently you simply buy them just because you can.

Struggling with anxiety means putting more intense pressure on yourself. If you're panicked and scared, it's easy to just go with the easiest and safest option. The intense pressure of all the "what if" thoughts can be so scary that it's best to just make a decision quickly rather than having to go through all those thoughts.

This struggle started a lot sooner than you were aware of. Reflect on your childhood. Your parents might have shown you that self-discipline was not a top priority to learn in your household. This could have been the way they dealt with problems, managed their health, or reached their goals. Even if you're nothing else like your parents now, the urge to push things back might have still been absorbed from them, now determining the way you act.

It simply feels good to give in to impulse because the hard stuff gets pushed until later. When presented with a challenge—like sticking to a goal—you have two options. Put in the work (like eating healthier, doing homework, cleaning, etc.) or just not and do it later. Our brains often like to choose the "do it later" option, but this ends up leaving us suffering worse later on. Self-discipline occurs when the temptation is subdued with the logic that you'll actually be better off in the end if you just do things right now.

Triggers, Impulses, and Self-Destruction

Triggers exist all around us. Sometimes, they are natural reminders, and other times, our brain clings to these triggers depending on the emotional state we were in before.

An impulse that many of us are very aware of is impulsive spending. This involves buying things that we don't need and not tracking properly how much money we are spending.

The impulse of many different things that we can buy exists around us in various forms. It can be something small, like impulsively buying a snack at the store that you don't need, or it could be a larger impulse, like getting a big house that you know you can't afford. The bigger the spend and the more impulsive the action, usually, the longer the negative outcome will be that we must deal with afterward. This can lead to buyer's remorse where we feel very regretful for spending our money in the first place.

Gambling is yet another impulse. This isn't just about money either; sometimes, we gamble with the circumstances. Knowing that a potentially bad outcome could happen is easily brushed aside when we act on an impulse because, usually, that desire and that urge are driven by a promise. Maybe a friend tells you about a business they have. They come to you extremely excited and hopeful about the outcome. They let you know with just a small couple thousand-dollar investment, your money will grow massively. This hope and excitement cause us to spend our money because we didn't give that decision enough time that it needed. We essentially gambled that money, which can be detrimental to our finances.

Sexual behavior can also be impulsive. There is nothing wrong with wanting to enjoy your sex life. However, some individuals might take this impulsive behavior to the next level. It could result in always hooking up with people and regretting it later on. Usually, the issue is when you act on that urge, rather than not properly planning something out.

Other forms of crime can also be impulsive. Deciding to swipe an item at the store or using recreational drugs are acts that we know we shouldn't do but will participate in any way. You might also have just a few drinks at the bar and think that you're fine to drive home at the end of the night, impulsively making a dangerous decision with consequences that could affect more than just you.

Changing things around rapidly can also be impulsive. Maybe you decide to cut and dye your hair a completely different color than anything you've ever done before. Maybe you impulsively paint rooms, rearrange furniture, buy a new car, switch apartments, or even change romantic partners frequently. Emotional eating is also often driven by an impulse. A deep emotional feeling that leads you to overcompensate by gorging on food can be an impulsive reaction that leads to more problems than were there initially.

Binge eating is its own psychological disorder, so it's a lot more than just impulse, but emotional eating is more common and can still occur in more people who are not properly managing those feelings.

Aggression is also a form of impulsive behavior. If somebody calls you a name and you decide to punch them in the face, that is you acting impulsively on those feelings.

While they might have "deserved" some sort of retribution for what they said, deciding that punishment in a split second can lead to more consequences than there were initially. By recognizing this impulsive behavior, it's easier to notice where you might struggle with your self-control.

Hey, it's Terry Lindberg,

As mentioned at the start of this book, you have an exclusive offer available to you for a short period of time.

In case you forgot to claim your 100% FREE, no strings attached ultimate mindset course by Intelligence Mastery.

Please can you make sure to do so NOW!

The reason for this is in the next coming chapters I will be discussing and referring back to parts of the course that Intelligence Mastery has created for you to improve your mindset.

It will be pivotal to have this course available at all times as when learning about self-improvement strategies, the ultimate mindset course will guide you to implement these strategies in a quick and effective manner.

In case you forgot how to claim your FREE copy of the Ultimate Mindset Course, search in your search browsers URL – free.intelligencemastery.com

Remember, before reading any further, please do this NOW as I will refer back to parts of the course throughout this book!

free.intelligencemastery.com

Chapter 3: Self-Discipline for Acquiring Healthy Habits

Though some level of self-discipline is natural in our lives, it's not an easy thing to build. Self-discipline is most simply acquired through creating smaller habits. Choosing to be more disciplined doesn't involve just one quick switch. Instead, it's a plan of action that includes multiple tinier steps to help get you there.

Habits require that you first notice them. Many habits become second nature to us, and we don't even think about them. Habits are everything from the way that you stand up and go to the bathroom to how you make your next decision. Habits are seen in the way that we walk, the way that we use our hands, the way that we talk to people, and the way that we interact. Some habits are more obvious in the way that we exercise or eat healthily.

There has to be a willingness to change when it comes to switching around your habits in a positive and beneficial way. A new habit commitment helps drive your urge to notice these bad habits and switch them around for the better.

Everything could be considered a habit if you break it down in the right way, so it's important for you to begin to train your brain to differentiate between the things that are habitual and healthy and the things that are actively harming you.

What Is a Habit?

A habit is a routine. We have habits because it's our brain's way of learning to do new things.

Imagine going to the bathroom and having to learn how to do so every single time. It might have taken a while for your parents to potty train you. As a parent yourself, you might also understand that it can be difficult to get a child to not only want to use the potty but to properly know how to do it. Habits are taught to us and imprinted in our brain, so the next time you have to repeat that action, it's second nature. If every time we had to go to the bathroom, we had to think about it and say, "Okay, I have to get it all out, get it all into the toilet, clean up properly afterward, flush, and walk away," as well as recognize signs and symptoms in our body that tell us to go to the bathroom in the first place, the world would be a very messed up place.

If this were the case, sometimes you might sit there and forget to go to the bathroom. You might not clean up well enough. These are all problems that children have, but as adults, we continue to learn healthier and more productive habits that create greater responsibility within ourselves.

Habits form our own behaviors and create the independent individuals that we are. They reflect how we're learning, and they show the way that we've been able to process information. These habits exist to help free up mental space. We don't have to think, "OK, how do I go to the bathroom, how do I brush my teeth, how do I take a shower, how do I cook breakfast, how do I drive a car to work?"

All of these things are second nature. You know that when cooking your eggs, you throw some butter in the pan, crack the eggs on top, mix them together with some onions and spinach, and serve them on your plate.

You don't have to sit there and think about any of that; it's all second nature to you. As you're doing this, you might be chatting to your kids or your spouse or just watching the news in the morning. You're going through these habits and not really thinking about them, and instead, they just become simple activities that are passing through time. This frees up your mental energy so that you can use it where you actually need it later on.

Things like critical thinking, analyzing, and other tasks that require your mental power will be easier to do because of the natural habits you've gone through.

Our habits are intertwined with each other. It's not just the act of doing something, but the situation that can also trigger different signals for habits within us.

For example, think about the Pavlovian theory. This is the idea that external sounds can be triggers to let you know that a certain habit is occurring. For example, a dog knows that it's time to eat not just because it's able to recognize the time of the day, but because it knows the different parts of the ritual that happen around eating. How many times have you opened a can of tuna, only for your cat to run into the room because it thinks that you're opening a can of its food? A sound can trigger a habit. Sometimes simply opening the fridge can also be a signal that now it's time to eat. These little minor rituals all add up to create that bigger habit.

Think about getting home from work and hearing your roommate open a beer. Walking through the door, being relieved that work is over, hearing the crack of the can, and seeing the time of the day all adds up and tells you, "Okay, now it's time to participate in the habit of having a beer after work."

If we're not careful, these habits can be harmful to us. These little rituals and signals and triggers can cause us to want to participate in bad or even damaging habits. How many times have you walked past the fridge and opened it even though you weren't planning on grabbing a snack? This is why becoming aware and paying attention to how we operate throughout the day is essential for helping us recognize the ways to inject self-discipline into our daily lives.

Examples of Common Bad Habits

One bad habit most of us know too well is pushing things off. Procrastination and avoiding our problems are common and natural because of that constant urge to not have to deal with our problems right away. We push things off like our work. We wait for later. We know that there's always going to be more time. We have to go back into work on Monday anyway, so we may as well save it for then.

We push off cleaning. We think about how it doesn't really matter if it's a mess. Who cares if the house is completely cluttered? No one sees it anyway.

We push off exercising. We think to ourselves, "I'll just start on Monday... I'll just start next week... I'll start when we get back from vacation..."

The thing about pushing things off is that it always makes things worse. Waiting until Monday to do your work means dreading your day going in on Monday. Pushing off cleaning means that the mess is even bigger, and now it's going to take you even longer. Pushing off exercising means you've gained more weight, so again, there's even more weight to manage, and now it's even harder to exercise than it would have been in the beginning.

To help recognize this bad habit, notice where your feelings of being overwhelmed are coming from. Are you overwhelmed because you have so much to clean in the kitchen? Are you feeling stressed out because you have too much work on your plate? Could you have done this sooner? Did you play an active role in pushing this off for later?

If so, look at the way you can change your language. Remove "later" as an option. Even if you can only contribute five minutes right now, that is still fine; habits build up from something small. Start with just working out for five minutes. Begin by just working on your homework for 10 minutes.

You might still stop, and that's fine because you at least put that effort in, so next time it's going to get easier. Tomorrow, work out for 10 minutes. Do homework for 20 minutes. Gradually increase things because it adds these habits more naturally so that you don't keep avoiding them and pushing them off.

Our eating habits are also often bad habits. We expect other people to sometimes make these decisions for us. Maybe you think,

"Well, my husband doesn't want to go vegan, so I can't." "My wife still brings home pizza from her job, so I can't go on my diet just yet." "My kids would never eat tofu, so I have to keep eating red meat every night."

Sometimes it's easy to pass the blame on to other people, but again, this is still within the bounds of our control. Ignoring your problems never makes them easier. This is another bad habit. Sometimes we ignore our health. We think, "Well I'm still young. I still have time. I'm healthier than some people I know at least!"

We also often ignore our feelings. We let people do things even if it makes us upset because it's easier to just deal with that than dealing with having to stand up for ourselves. We ignore our feelings and pretend like everything is fine and go on as normal because we don't want anything to change.

Don't ignore these habits anymore. Don't wait around for somebody else. Don't cast the blame onto somebody else, and now more than ever, it's important that we face our issues and embrace and accept that reality.

Overthinking is also a bad habit. We can easily get stuck and lost by ruminating and going over the same thoughts repeatedly. Maybe you can't help but think about what other people think of you. Maybe you're worried about judgment. Maybe you overthink about overthinking in general! Maybe you wonder if you're making the right decisions. It's important to be analytical, but remember that there is a fine line. If you find the same thoughts are repeating and nothing is really changing, it's a sign that you're overthinking.

This can often increase anxiety and lead to another bad habit that is acting on impulse. This is aggression with others. It's making irrational decisions. It's doing things that will negatively impact you later on because you're feeling fear right now.

Once you start to recognize these bad habits in your life, it's easier to implement methods to break them.

How Can Someone Break Habits?

The first step to break these habits is to identify the impulse that is causing you to act out in the first place. What fear is driving you? What anxiety exists behind this? Is there an underlying passion or pressure or stress that is leading to these impulses?

Look at any sort of past trauma or feelings that you are not managing. Are they manifesting themselves through your habits?

For example, if you had a very bad emotional relationship with somebody in the past, whether you were neglected or abused, it's easy to suppress these feelings and, instead, act impulsively now as a way to alleviate them. If you struggled with emotional abuse, you might find that you have an addiction now. Perhaps drinking alcohol or binge eating is a way to sort of numb or at least release some of the pressure that these feelings bring.

Impulses can also be anxiety over the future. Are you making irrational decisions just because you are scared of where you're going to end up later on? Maybe you have dreams of becoming really successful one day, but things just haven't been happening for you so far, so you're making impulsive decisions like buying lottery tickets all the time or investing in risky businesses, always trying to find a way to climb to the top.

By noticing what these impulses are driven by, it's easier to discover methods to overcome them. When breaking habits, have a goal. Why is this habit bad for you and what benefit will there be in the end if you do manage to break that habit?

As you are implementing this practice, make sure to have a healthy habit to replace the bad one.

If you are eating unhealthily all the time, don't just stop eating. Instead, pick healthier options. You're still going to have cravings at night and have impulses, so instead of trying to go cold turkey and force yourself to not think about that food, let yourself still eat, just pick something better. Instead of eating an entire gallon of ice cream, can you have some fruit in your fridge? Can you have a mini-sized candy bar?

Every time that you take a habit away, you're taking away something that you're comfortable with. It's a natural ritual that you have in your life, and once that is removed, it causes stress and panic. We become dependent on our habits as a constant thing in our life.

This is why it's so hard to go cold turkey. Once we take that away, our minds freak out for a minute and think, "Oh my god, what are we going to do? You just took away this thing that made us feel good!"

Even if it had negative side effects later on, your brain doesn't always realize that. If you're giving up smoking because you don't want lung cancer, your brain thinks to itself, "I love smoking; it makes me feel good every time we have a cigarette."

Even though you go inside and that cigarette is gone and you feel like crap, your brain is going to associate a good feeling with the cigarette since that was the initial relief.

Now you've taken that away, and your brain is wondering, "What are we going to do? I need that thing to feel good."

This is why you have to have something to replace it with so that you're distracted and less likely to return to that negative habit. Instead of having a cigarette, you can have an exercise bike in the basement that you go to and work out for 10 minutes, the same amount of time that it would take you to go outside and smoke a cigarette. Your brain then thinks, "Wow, exercising makes me feel good."

You are distracted. You've pulled away from your work, and you have regulated your breathing. Your brain is still going to want to have that cigarette, but it's easier to fight through that impulse when you've provided something else that makes you feel good.

When you're breaking these habits, track your progress to notice how things have changed. What have been more weaknesses along the way? For example, you might know that lunch breaks at work are very triggering for you to want to have a cigarette. These are moments of weakness, so you have to be even more prepared to fight those feelings off.

You can start taking a different time for lunch breaks. You can go somewhere different, you can go for a drive, or you can have a lunchtime treat. Whatever you do, replace that habit with something else as you identify these weaknesses along the way.

Examples of Healthy Habits to Emulate

Always start sooner. It's true that time is limited in our world, but it doesn't have to feel like that every single day. While you might not think you have 10 minutes to spare when looking at your schedule, you will always save at least that much extra time. We can't always contribute three-hour blocks to a task like cleaning out the closet, but you could give it 10 minutes a day, and after two weeks, it could be a completely new closet. Don't look at tasks as huge things to do all at once, and instead, look for small ways to insert these habits where you can.

Take care of yourself first. Though it feels selfish sometimes, if you're not taking care of yourself, you're just depleting your ability to help or take care of others! We can't give from an empty basket, so remind yourself of the importance of checking in with your own needs rather than only focusing on those of others. Don't overexert yourself to the point you're constantly taking on tasks but never slowing down to really embrace your own life.

Be more patient. Time does seemingly run out so quickly, but remember to enjoy those moments that are slow. Success takes time to build. Only after a certain amount of time are we able to see true change. Though having and keeping up with this kind of patience can be difficult, it's an important part of self-control.

Don't feel rushed, and keep trying after you've failed. If you fail at something you tried, it's easy to want to start over and move on to a new method. However, sometimes we can retry things and get different results, so remember that going through the same process might make you feel stressed, anxious, and rushed, but it can still be quicker than starting over with something else. Failing multiple times over and over again is a sign you should move on, but remember to not get scared after the initial moment something bad happens.

Show gratitude. Many people have a bad habit of never being satisfied. It's easy and natural to do. You might be eating a tasty meal and then think, "If only it had this..." Maybe everything went well during a party, but you can't help but think, "Next time I'll do this better." It's OK to be critical for improvement, but don't let that judgment turn ugly and take away from the event. Rather than being worried about what you don't have, show appreciation and thankfulness for the things you do have.

Learn more. Try new things. Keep an open mind. Admit when you're wrong. Listen to others. These things help us grow. Has anyone ever taken away from their life by learning more? Expand what you already know, and find out things you don't already have knowledge of. Explore areas you didn't know existed, and get excited about learning. By giving yourself this advantage, you're creating a healthier and happier life surrounding continual upward expansion.

Chapter 4: Increasing Mental and Emotional Strength for Happiness

Implementing methods to incorporate strength training your mind is just as important as doing so for your body. We put pressure on ourselves to work out at the gym, but not everyone is as concerned with making sure their mind has the same kind of energy.

Notice your thoughts more. Challenge the beliefs that you simply let pass through your mind. Stop and think, "Where did that thought come from?"

Be aware of the thoughts that have been controlling your emotions. The situation doesn't have to change how you feel. It's your mind that plays the biggest role in how you feel. I've helped clients from many different walks of life. Some had financial struggles and others didn't have to worry about money for the majority of their life.

Managing Emotions

Anger, frustration, guilt, and regret can all be very hard emotions to manage. They create these constant thoughts in our brains that become difficult to overcome. While self-discipline might seem like it's just about avoiding lazy tendencies and putting more effort in, it actually revolves around managing these emotions.

Understand the difference between your response and reaction. Whenever you feel something, it starts with a reaction. This is mostly out of our control. If someone says something rude to you, you'll likely react with shock. Your response then comes after. You can use this feeling to respond by saying something rude back. You can respond by walking away. You can respond by having a civil discussion and talking about how they hurt your feelings.

Our reaction is in our control, but that's certainly harder to manage. It's understandable that a rude comment would hurt your feelings. It's how you respond to that reaction that matters the most. Those with a high level of self-control can walk away and not cause more damage, but those with no self-control will lash out and use violence in that situation.

Avoid taking things too personally. Remain neutral and objective to your feelings. Remind yourself that how you feel doesn't have to be a fact for how the situation is. It's common to have certain reactions depending on the situation, but again, these don't have to determine exactly how you'll interact in that scenario.

Sometimes you just have to embrace your feelings—good or bad. What matters more than anything is ensuring you're doing your best to keep those responses under your control. When you feel an emotion, stop and question it. Ask, "Is this right? Is this feeling true? Is this something that is entirely within my control? What are my options when reacting to this situation? What choices can I make that might determine where I end up?"

The Key to Self-Confidence

To increase your self-confidence, it's important to pay attention to the way you're talking to yourself. If you were babysitting two children and one started calling the other names, you'd likely stop them and tell them it's mean. However, when we start calling ourselves names, that same kind of discipline goes away. Instead of reminding ourselves it's mean and we shouldn't call ourselves ugly, dumb, or a loser, we buy into this and begin to believe it's true. This can end up completely destroying our self-confidence.

Self-confidence can sometimes feel like it's just how others treat us. Having a bully constantly belittle you is a surefire way to feel like you're a bad person. While this does contribute to how we feel, it's not the only definitive determination for our self-confidence. You could have 100 bullies or 100 fans; either situation doesn't mean you are free from anxiety and filled with self-confidence.

Notice the definitive statements that you're making to yourself. If you mess up once, it's easy to think you're an instant failure. Would you believe the same thing of someone else? If we have one bad hair day, it's easy to feel like we're ugly or unattractive. Would you tell that to someone you loved who was having issues with their self-confidence?

Understand why it's so unfair to make comparisons. We hold ourselves to the highest judgment. The key to self-confidence is to begin by ensuring you're not being too hard on yourself. Don't hold yourself up to a harsh comparison that you wouldn't hold someone else to. Why is it fair for you to do that to yourself but not to others?

Comparison is hard to overcome, but it's an area to be more disciplined in. Think about social media. It's easy to look at friends and feel envious that you don't have what they do. You might see them posting with friends, a partner, or even their children and think to yourself, "They're perfect, but I'm not. Why?" It's easy to create a perspective on social media to have others believe one side of the truth. It is true they are a happy family. It's not always true that things are perfect. They might have moments where their children freak out, they cry and fight, and things just feel too hard to handle. People don't post this on social media as often, however. Remind yourself of this when you get stuck in a comparison loop. What about the truth are you forgetting? What aspects might you be ignoring when making this comparison? Be disciplined with your thoughts and remember to not buy too deep into the lies you're telling yourself.

Increasing Focus and Attention

Recognize distractions. The number one thing that keeps us from focusing is our mind, but the more distractions around us, the more fuel for this inability to pay attention. If you're anything like me, you could be in a blank white room with no access to the internet and still find a way to struggle with focus.

However, the first thing to do is to remove these distractions to make it easier to keep your mind disciplined. Start with physical clutter. This is things like stacks of unread books, projects you've never finished, and messes piling up. Even though you don't sit there and necessarily stare at these things the whole time you're trying to work, your brain is likely still picking up on these things and storing the memories in the back of your mind.

Notifications also take a lot of our focus away. Again, even though you're not actively sitting there texting someone, the notification that you're getting messages might pull your attention. You could go an hour without checking, but the thoughts of, "I wonder what the message says," can swirl through your brain.

Turn off notifications whenever you have to focus to start. Simply shut your phone or the volume off.

Consider turning notifications off from your phone altogether. If someone really needs you in an emergency, they will call you. Facebook, Instagram, Twitter, and other social media don't really require your constant attention.

To take things a step further for your concentration, create a "focus" object. I like to use a notecard, but your object can be anything you want. Keep this within the range of your vision as you're working. If you start to gaze out the window, get tempted by your phone, or simply "zone out," your visual reminder will be there to get back to work.

Overall, include more "focus workouts" in your day-to-day routine. Pick puzzles like sudoku, crosswords, or word searches. These can help train your mentality to be more analytical and focused when you need to be.

Chapter 5: Willpower and Weight Loss

Gaining the means to lose weight doesn't have to be a challenge. Self-discipline is required because it's what can be used to overcome those urges to give in to cravings. The things that have been preventing us from losing weight can all be combated by increasing our willpower.

Of course, there will always be underlying health conditions that have the potential to contribute to a struggle with weight, but much of our health still lies within the bounds of our control.

Accessibility is a big contributing factor to why it's so challenging to manage our health. It's easy to drive through somewhere and get a 1,000+ calorie meal for less than $5. It's simple to order these kinds of treats directly to your doorstep!

The more that you think about something, the harder it can be to avoid it. If you have to tell yourself to repeatedly not think about all the snacks in your cupboard or eating the rest of your meal prep, you're going to want to do it even more.

Making healthy food, going to the gym, and doing other things to lose weight isn't easy. These require time and patience, and that's a crucial part of maintaining a high level of self-discipline for your health.

Why Is It So Hard to Lose Weight?

There are many setbacks that keep us from losing weight. Stress is a huge part. A lot of this stress also comes about because we aren't properly managing our thoughts in the first place. For example, you might have started a diet successfully on a Sunday. By Tuesday, you've given in to a craving after ignoring your thoughts. Then on Wednesday, you decide, "Whatever, my diet is already ruined, so I may as well give in and eat more sweets."

By feeling like a failure and struggling with your self-control surrounding these things, you likely become focused on ruminating on that stress. If you repeatedly fail and are hard on yourself each time, you start to feel like a failure. Then you act on those feelings, giving up and ignoring your health. How is anyone supposed to work hard to take care of their body if they don't think they're worth it in the first place?

Our biology certainly plays a part in working against us as well. It's easy to give in to natural cravings and urges because your brain will convince you it's what is needed. If you're used to eating whatever you want whenever, then your brain isn't going to just stop craving these types of foods just because you're trying to diet. It's used to a pattern, so once you take that comfort of unhealthy food away, your brain panics, making it even harder to resist these cravings.

Losing weight requires three major parts of your mental abilities:

1. Emotional management
2. Behavior
3. Attention

First and foremost, you will be required to manage your emotions. It's hard to have a healthy body if you don't have a healthy mind.

Your behavior then becomes a result of this management. How are you able to ignore these challenging thoughts to keep your health's best interest in mind first?

Finally, attention and emphasis should be placed on losing weight. You should want to lose weight for the right reasons while also creating goals to follow. It's not going to happen naturally. Getting healthier doesn't occur like magic. It's your responsibility, so it will require attention and passion toward it to become happier and healthier in the end.

Cravings and Impulses

By taking something away, it instantly becomes more desirable in your mind. If I told you not to read the next sentence, you'd only want to read it more. Pretty tempting to just keep reading, right?

The expectations of the food you're eating drive the passion to want to partake in the enjoyment of certain foods. If you're sitting there trying to not think about walking down the block to your favorite restaurant and ordering dinner, you're going to want to think of it more, and it will also end up becoming more desirable. Any other day, you might just walk and grab food without thinking about it. But now this normal activity is more desirable because you're building it up. You're "not" thinking about the way the food tastes, smells, and makes you feel. You're focusing on every little detail, making one small thing turn into something way bigger than it should be. How can anyone be expected to then resist these cravings with such a big temptation?

Once we give in to one thing, it makes it harder to stop because of the heightened gratification. If you told yourself, "OK, I can have just one piece of candy," after trying to avoid it all day, that piece of candy will taste so much better than any other normal day. That reward is huge for your mentality, meaning you'll want to eat another to feel that same effect. Even though we're acting impulsively, our brains are still feeling the reward.

This is why starvation will never work. It might seem more "disciplined" to just not eat, but in reality, you're just making eating even more desirable. To practice true willpower is to be able to face these foods and eat smaller portions or choose healthier options.

Don't deprive yourself because it just makes things harder. In fact, overload yourself at the start. Once you switch from unhealthy eating to a healthier alternative, start by not limiting your portions so much. A huge salad might be too big of a meal, but it's still better than binging fast food. As time goes on, you can decrease the portion. The point is to just ensure you're not starting with deprivation or else you'll be desiring those "forbidden" foods even more.

Self-Discipline Tips for Weight Loss

One place to start is with the use of affirmations. We often say negative things to ourselves, and it's hard to not believe that they are the truth. A positive affirmation can help turn around those negative thoughts so you are more likely to believe these types of phrases:

- I am brave.
- I am powerful.
- I am passionate.
- I am healthy.

Of course, just saying these affirmations isn't an instant fix, but the more you start to add these to your self-vocabulary, the more normal they become.

Remember to take care of your health overall. Losing weight isn't just to make you look good. In fact, you can be underweight and unhealthy or appear overweight but actually be healthy. If you ignore your health and only care to lose weight for your external appearance, it will be easier to make bad choices that go against anything that could help.

Remember that the more repetition you put toward your goals, the easier it is for them to be natural. It might seem like if you fail, you should give up, but ask how much progress you made. Even if it's small, on the next try it might be bigger, so keep pushing forward.

Chapter 6: Excelling in Your Career With Self-Discipline

Work doesn't have to be a painful experience. It should be our passion! That doesn't mean it doesn't get hard from time to time. We all have moments where we wish we were home, and you might even go as far as to question if you've followed the wrong life purpose up until this point.

Work can put a lot of pressure on our lives and seems to have control over many of our emotions. Self-discipline means creating boundaries both inside and outside of work, as well as the barriers in between when those time periods crossover.

Work Weaknesses

What area of work do you feel requires more self-discipline from you?

For many, procrastination is one of the biggest issues. Not only is it hard to get work done, but your professional advancement might depend on you creating goals and sticking to them to see greater results.

Sometimes, work is hard because we take things too personally. An inability to take constructive criticism can come from not managing your emotional responses.

Letting stress overwhelm us, not trying hard enough, or even trying too hard can result in overexertion and impatience with change.

The first step is to recognize these areas of weakness so you can create actionable plans to overcome them. Where are you struggling now and what methods can be implemented to help in the future?

Setting Goals

Don't wait around for things to get rolling. Your first step should be to create more realistic goals. Don't expect to go from entry-level to CEO in a year. Be more honest with yourself and your ability to actually follow through with these plans.

Don't depend on things you can't control. Don't bank on your boss being in a good mood. Don't expect things will happen naturally (raises/advancements). Remember the things you have power over and to differentiate from what is simply in the hands of others.

Take more initiative and never expect someone else to get things done. While you can't have control over everything, you can always seek out ways to use your power of influence in smaller methods.

Gradually increase your goals as you go along, and always check back in with your progress. Any of the methods of self-discipline we talked about throughout the book can be beneficial for you to use going forward.

To recap, remember:

- Create realistic goals
- Don't depend on things you can't control
- Take more initiative
- Track your goals and see how you can improve
- Gradually make things harder and goals bigger

From a more practical standpoint, stick to these tips:

1. Start on a Sunday. You can still relax and enjoy your day off while also planning and preparing for Monday. Starting while already behind will only make it harder to catch up.
2. Practice different ways to say, "NO." Sometimes, you'll have to delegate tasks more properly that you can't do, and this might mean turning work projects down. You can still do this in a productive way without jeopardizing your progression.
3. Be excited about every challenge. No matter how big the obstacle, it will still present a way for you to learn.
4. Use positivity. Work is simply just boring, stressful, or menial sometimes. The only way to deal with this is to get through it, so you may as well try to look on the positive side rather than always choosing negativity.

Hey, it's Terry Lindberg,

Firstly thanks for completing my book this should set you up for success by putting you on the right path.

Remember, there are particular tools that you need not just to make your self-improvement journey easier, but make it more effective.

The first crucial tool you will need to make sure you have, so you do not fail, is the Ultimate Mindset Course by Intelligence Mastery.

As when starting your journey of self-improvement, the one thing that anybody who reaches success has; is a detailed plan in place.

To create a detailed plan to have a mindset shift that you'll need to set you up for success; you have to do endless amounts of research to get mental clarity, acquire new daily habits, and much more.

Sounds like hard work, right?

Well yes, it would be, but luckily for you, I have partnered up with Intelligence Mastery. Who are giving away their highly rated course that will give you all of the step-by-step process for shifting your mindset into gear seamlessly!

Best thing about this exclusive offer is it 100% FREE, no-strings-attached. Intelligence Mastery usually charge $297 for this exact same course to their customers

Make sure to search in on your browsers URL – free.intelligencemastery.com

Good luck on your journey and enjoy the course!

free.intelligencemastery.com

Conclusion

You're in charge of your level of self-discipline. No matter how many triggers and temptations you face on a daily basis, it will still be you at the end of the day who decides whether or not to give in to these things. Some days will be harder than others, but you're the leader, captain, chief, and person in charge of your emotions and actions.

There will always be some setbacks. Unexpected things challenge us in ways we never thought possible. Unforeseen circumstances present obstacles we don't have a plan to overcome. This is OK! Preparation isn't always necessary and instead, managing your emotions to build stronger reactions can help more than being ready with a plan of action. While you might not be expecting everything to fall apart, you can still be mentally prepared to work through this if it does occur.

The increase in your mental strength means increasing your intelligence. Sometimes you just have to avoid triggers rather than being strong enough to face them, and that's OK! It shows you're being logical and realistic with yourself.

What matters most is returning to yourself and your needs after all is said and done. Continue to check in with yourself to ensure you are probably nurturing your needs.

The only person you're hurting by being self-"rebellious" is yourself. You can say, "Screw it, I'm going to eat that extra slice. I don't care about the rules of my diet." That's fine. No one is going to punish you. The only negative results will directly affect you. Remind yourself that you're only causing personal damage when choosing to be self-destructive.

Check out other books in the series to continue to grow your knowledge. The more areas you study mental health, the easier it will be for you to build the strength needed to overcome the biggest internal roadblocks.

Continue this discussion by leaving a review as well! Psychology, in general, is based in science, and that's important to remember, but a huge part also revolves around perception and the individual experience. For this reason, any thoughts and tips to share and discuss are always welcome. Not only does it help you and me, but it also helps all of those who participate in these kinds of discussions.

The journey of self-discovery never quite stops. There isn't any endpoint to work for but instead, an appreciation required to enjoy every step of the way.

If you found this book useful in anyway, an honest review is always appreciated!